I Still Believe in

Santa Claus

(Only for Grown Ups)

Darren Griffin

Other works by Darren Griffin

Unlocking Your Potential through Self Hypnosis

How to be a Ventriloquist

Micro-Nap: The Five Minute Rejuvenation (audio cd)

Ventriloquism, Fatherhood and Bunny Buttons: An Autobiography Part 1

Glimpses into the Darkness: A Collection of Short Horror Stories

Echoes of the Darkness: Another Collection of Short Horror Stories

Standing Room Only: Yet Another Collection of Short Horror Stories

Chess: The Game of Humiliating Both Friends and Strangers

Peace Amidst Misunderstanding: Living and Thriving With Mental Illness

This is Me!

Duncan MacSanchez and the Blaze of Glory, and Other Stories

Titanicus the Barbarian

Titanicus and the Amulet of Time

Titanicus and the Children of Thunder

God Lives, and I Can Prove It

The Big Green Forest, a Collection of Bedtime Stories

Rednecks vs. UFOs

Moods: An Album of Meditative Music (audio)

ISBN-13: 978-1502551788

ISBN-10: 1502551780

Dedication

Part of the magic of Christmas is seeing the bright eyes of children as they await the coming of Santa. That light dims as they grow older and are told "THE TRUTH".

It is with the hope of reigniting that light in the eyes and hearts of disillusioned children of all ages that this book is written.

WARNING: This book is for those who have been told that there is no Santa. It contains spoilers that young children will not appreciate.

Contents

Acknowledgments

This little book owes it's existence to my father, I suppose. All throughout his life he held fast to his belief in Santa Claus. Seeing this I delved into my own believes and found I believe in Santa also, but for a little different reason.

So in a world of skepticism, and behavior worthy of coal in the stockings, here's some things to think about.

Here's a few reasons you can believe in Santa Claus again.

1 Memories of Childhood

I was born at a very young age in a hospital my parents had not planned on going to. The hospital they wanted to go to was on the other side of town and during the frantic drive in mid September my father encountered a number of one way streets he had never seen before. This eventually deposited them in front of the unknown but, luckily, very competent facility.

As Christmas came 'round I was too involved with trying to hold up my head and figure out what my fingers were for to really pay it much attention.

By my third Christmas I was starting to get the idea and Christmas Eve became the longest day of the year and the hardest to get to sleep on.

Why hard to get to sleep? Because Santa was coming! All the shows on television said so. So did the music on the radio and my dad's records. (Big black circular things that made noise. Kind of like CDs. Small silver circular things that made noise.)

My family consisted of me and my parents. My grandparents, aunts and uncles and so forth all lived far away and were unable to visit except for a week or so during the summer. As it turned out I was fated to be an only child, so the happy memories of running to the Christmas Tree with brothers and sisters were never to be mine, however, I've watched enough television to know what that must be like.

Throughout the years Santa brought me toy dinosaurs, bows and arrows, cap guns, walkie talkies, puzzles and lots of hard candy that was really hard to break apart, especially the kind that came in multicolored ribbons. If you've had it you know what I mean.

For the first few years we had real trees, although I can't remember where they came from. Picturing the three of us plowing through the snow, somewhere far from a television set, in search of the perfect tree seems as likely as an Emperor Penguin showing up to fix my dishwasher.

When I was five I remember going with my mother down to the department store to get an artificial tree. I don't know which store it was because everyone just called it "The Department Store". On a display stand she found a tree she liked. I remember she was proud of herself because she only paid eight dollars for it.

We got it home and drug the box, which was bigger than I was, into the front room. The plain white cardboard gave no indication of the wondrous glory inside. My dad pulled off the tape running down the middle and we carefully and excitedly opened the lid as if it were the sarcophagus of some ancient pharaoh. Inside were two poles, an instruction sheet, and a vast array of large "branches" of various sizes. These were actually green wires with plastic pine needles sticking out of them. We put the two poles together and thus made the trunk. The instruction sheet drew our attention to the fact that the "branches" were color coded, as were the holes in the "trunk". This allowed us to know which holes the various lengths of spiky wire went into.

As we worked the tree began to take shape and became far more than the sum of the parts. Once the lights (always my dad's job) and decorations were on, it's blazing glory became the center of our holiday festivities.

It's been forty years since my mother paid her eight dollars. My parents have passed away and the house was sold long ago, but the tree now stands in the front room of my home. My children have helped assemble it every year of their lives and it is a part of their Christmas memories and heritage.

Mom knew how to pick 'em.

And now it was Christmas Eve. The day had been interminable. As bedtime approached we hung up our stockings, put out milk and cookies on a plate (maybe some carrots for his reindeer) and sang carols around the new artificial tree. We talked about the meaning of Christmas, I got to open one present and then it was off to bed.

You know the deal. If you stay up too late Santa might have to miss your house.

We turned off the lights in the front room and trudged upstairs. I knew sleep was far away. My dad could never sleep on Christmas Eve either so he came into my room and told me some bed time stories about Mickey Monkey and the Big Green Forest.

From downstairs came a noise. It was not the arising of such a clatter, but it was a noise. Both of us heard it.

"Maybe we should go see," my five year old self said.

My dad agreed, so we opened my door and peered out into the hall. My mom was coming out of her room also.
Looking down the stairs I could see that the lights were back on. We descended and the front room was a Christmas miracle. The stockings were filled! Presents were under the tee that hadn't been there a few minutes ago. Standing in plain sight was an action figure I had asked Santa for weeks earlier!

Strangest of all, the front door was ajar and I almost think I caught the briefest glimpse of a white ball on the end of a red hat as if someone were just running out the door.

There was no going back to bed now and my parents said I could stay up and play with whatever was unwrapped. They wearily climbed the stairs and went to bed, but my new action figure kept me busy until four in the morning. I don't remember if I went to bed then or just fell asleep under the tree, but it was the greatest Christmas of my five year old life.

2 Evidence

I was eight years old. My life was dominated by the third grade and the nightmarish torments it held.

One of the bright points of the year, Halloween had just ended. I always loved that season of imagination and pretend, although my mother would always ruin my costume by making me *wear a coat over it*. The inhumanity. Moms just don't understand that boys would rather look scary and get pneumonia that stay healthy and look "Cute".

Now it was time to turn our thoughts to Thanksgiving. I love the holiday now, but as a kid I thought it was exciting only because it was the gateway to Christmas. Thanksgiving is like the food of Christmas but without any other benefits. No toys, and no TV specials. Just football--which held as much interest to me as a yawn marathon at an encyclopedia factory. (An encyclopedia is a book with a bunch of information in it, like the internet on paper.)

The significance of this time of year to an eight year old was this: Department store catalogues began showing up in the mail.

These were not mere brochures or flyers, these were extensive catalogues that were several inches thick. Within their pages could be found everything a boy or girl could possibly want for Christmas. Imagine Amazon in book form.

Armed with a red magic marker I would go through their pages and circle those items I had never known about but suddenly could not live without. A turned down page was also appropriate on really important items.

I would then turn the book of wonders over to my mother and through a secret process I was never to fully understand, she got the information to Santa who put some of the items under the tree on Christmas Eve. Of course I would see Santa at the church Christmas party and speak with him from the lofty height of his knee, but he was usually vague about whether I would get the items or not.

This year as I turned past page after page of desirable merchandise I found a treasure trove. One full page was dedicated to ventriloquist figures. I was familiar with ventriloquism from listening to my father's old time radio collection.

I knew my search was over. This is what I wanted Santa to bring me.

There were many to choose from, some I had seen before, some I hadn't. I picked one I was unfamiliar with and gave it a big circle with my marker. I also turned down the page. This was serious business.

I gave the catalogue to my mother, pointing out the most important page, and felt assured she would send the document through the appropriate channels.

Life continued. We made turkeys in class. They gave us color sheets with Indians and Pilgrims both happy and smiling. Apparently the Indians were unaware that the Whiteman was about to stick it to them.

Thanksgiving came and went and the playground conversations turned to Santa and hoped for presents. Most of us were of the opinion that Santa was real, but there were a misguided few who tried to tell us it was all made up. Poor lost souls, we thought. Probably poor upbringing.

Proof abounded. The disappearing milk and cookies. The appearing presents. The filled stockings. The various television shows that featured Santa. All the music about the man in red.

In the face of such overwhelming evidence I expected their disbelief to crumble, but still they doubted.

I would relate some of these conversations to my dad and he assured me that he still believed in Santa Claus.

The signs of Christmas' approach began to appear. Our tree was assembled and decorated. Wreaths and bows began to pop up around town. We cut out snow flakes in school.

The days rolled by slowly, as they always do prior to Christmas.

The heretics at school became more outspoken.

Finally the last day of school ended and I raced home filled with the exuberance Christmas vacation brings.

As Christmas Eve Day finally dawned I played in the snow, looked at the clock, played in my room, looked at the clock. Went back outside, looked at the clock.

At long last it was lunch time.

Each hour of the afternoon lasted three or four. Finally the sun began to set and a nervous anticipation crept over me. Santa's visit was drawing nigh.

We followed our usual traditions. Put out the goodies, hung the stockings, read about the birth of Christ from Luke chapter two and sang carols around the tree. I opened my one present, but don't remember what it was, so anxious was I to see what the morning would bring.

I trundled off to bed where I lay in the darkness, willing myself to sleep. It was a long time before I finally drifted off.

My dad had trouble sleeping on Christmas Eve as well and would watch the clock. When the morning came and he felt it was time to start opening presents he would slide out of bed, put on his slippers and a button up sweater over his pajamas and go into the kitchen where he would "accidentally" start dropping pots and pans on the floor.

It was this cacophony that woke me. Then the realization hit me. It was Christmas Morning! I had made it through the interminable night! I bounced out of bed as if fired from a catapult.

Both my parents were up, my mom having investigated the tumult in the kitchen, and were waiting for me.

I ran to the tree and saw that Santa had brought me a. . . rocking chair. Sitting in the chair was my ventriloquist figure! Leaning against the chair was a record of instructions for talking without moving your lips.

My dad pulled his sweater down over his belly, where it immediately began to ride back up over the bulge, and said: "Looks like Santa came!" He took his stocking over to the couch, plopped, and began to rummage through it.

My mother perused the contents of hers, but I had eyes only for this piece of magic whose name was Danny.

From the couch my mother said: "Who wants to play Santa this year?"

I was voted the honor and began handing out presents.

"One at a time so everyone can see," my mom said. She had a pencil and notebook in hand, ready to write everything down so the "Thank You Notes" could commence.

Each scrap of wrapping paper was jammed into a garbage sack, and soon all the presents were unwrapped, and placed in piles around their respective owners.

I placed presents into two categories. Everything Fun and Clothes. Once my system failed because I got a Batman costume. I put it into the Everything Fun category even though it technically belonged in Clothes.

I turned my attention back to Danny. I took

him and the record to my room. I noticed that he had a pull string coming out of the back of his neck that would open his mouth when pulled. I put the record on my small turntable and became a ventriloquist.

I was the only ventriloquist in the third grade and the teacher asked me to come do a show for class. I did, and it was a hit.

I've continued to practice ventriloquism ever since. I now have 14 characters and do shows all over the western United States. Although Danny is no longer part of my show, he hangs out in my office and gives me inspiration.

I did a number of shows for my elementary school. Each time I was asked where I got Danny from I would say "Santa". This caused consternation from some, admiration from others and arguments from the heretics.

I knew the truth. Santa came through for me and changed my life.

3 Finding the Forbidden

It was a Saturday in March and I was on a quest for candy. My mom would occasionally pull out a box of bird shaped suckers and impart of one to my eight year old self. They weren't the greatest, but they were sugar. I never knew where she kept them, and since she wasn't around at the moment, I decided to find them.

This led me to drawers and cupboards I had never before investigated. I didn't ever find the suckers, but I did find something else. A dinosaur model, brand new and still sealed in the box. I was looking at the back of the box, on which the wonders of the model were printed for all to see, when my mother appeared in the doorway.

Excited to show off my find, I began to tell her

all about it. The expression on her face was not one of excitement, but frustration with a little anger mixed in.

"Darn it honey," she said. "I was going to give that to you for Easter."

I didn't follow her logic.

"That's OK," I said. "The Easter Bunny will bring me something. Don't worry about it."

"What I'm telling you," she said slowly, "Is this is what you are getting for Easter."

Being equally patient I said "And I'm telling you not to worry because the Easter Bunny will take care of things. The Easter Bunny."

I didn't know why she wasn't getting this. I'd had seven Easters and she should know how it works by now.

She looked at me with a puzzled expression and then said the words that changed my life: "You don't still believe in that, do you?"

"In what?" I was still not following.

SPOILER ALERT!!!!!!!

"I'm the one that puts the things in your Easter Basket. I thought you knew that."

What madness was this?

I felt a small degree of shock, but then it kind of made sense. The idea of a giant bunny merrily hopping about the house holding a basket filled with colored eggs and toys seemed suspect in the least and possibly downright eerie.

I decided I could accept this.

"I guess that's OK," I said to my mom. "At least we know that Santa is real." I smiled.

She didn't smile.

BIGGER SPOILER ALERT!!!

"I put the toys under the tree as well."

BLAM!!!!

My heart dropped to the floor and exploded. My mom was on the side of the heretics!! How could she be so misguided?! Then I thought: "What if it's all true? What if there's no Santa Claus? What else had they told me that wasn't true? What about God? Was He like Santa? Merely something parents tell their children?"

What fresh new hell had I stepped into?

I no longer knew what to believe. Everything my parents had told me became suspect. My world was rocked.

My mother seemed rather nonchalant about the whole thing, but I was not. The people I trusted most had **lied** to me.

I stumbled out of the room, my eight year old legs wobbly, in search of my dad. The man who "believed" in Santa.

Let's hear what he had to say now!

4 My Dad's Explanation

I found him in his usual place in the basement, surrounded by his records and tapes. I told him about my conversation with mom and the horrible secrets that had been revealed. I ended by saying: "You told me you believed in Santa Claus!" I almost yelled.

He replied calmly: "I said that because I do."

"Well," I said calming down a little. "How's that work?"

"I believe that Santa Claus is a name given to people who give to others. Especially if they give in love. As long as parents give gifts to their children there will always be a Santa Claus. When you give a gift to your mother, even if it's a gift of service and not a tangible present, you are being a Santa Claus."

I thought about this.

"So," I said at length. "There's not just one Santa Claus? Anybody who gives to another person gets to be a Santa Claus?"

"That's exactly right," he said. "On Christmas morning when you "Play Santa" by handing out the gifts, you really are being a Santa."

My belief in Santa was returning with this new description. I understood what my dad was saying and in the light of this new concept I could say I believed in Santa Claus once more. Even though it was my mother who put Danny under the tree, she was giving a gift of love, which made her a Santa. So Santa actually had brought Danny.

My mind was stretching with this new concept and I went back out into the March sunshine armed with a little wisdom and, although it was different than it had been, a belief in Santa Claus.

5 My Own Explanation

My dad continued to believe in this concept of Santa Claus for the rest of his life.

I am a researcher by nature and I continued to explore the concept and philosophy of Santa.

Recently my wife came home from church, I had stayed in bed nursing a cold. She came into the bedroom and told me that a good part of class had been taken up by the question: Do we do a disservice to Christ when we talk about Santa?

Many of the parents felt guilty talking about Santa and taking their children to see him because the Christmas holiday should center around Christ.

This subject comes up every year.

Let's look at the characteristics of Santa Claus.

- He rewards those children who are good.
- He loves everyone.
- He wears red.
- His hair and beard are white as snow.

He symbolizes Christmas and the birth of the Saviour of the world.

Now let's look at the characteristics of Christ Himself.

- He rewards the righteous. (Matthew 16:37)
- Loves everyone. (John 13:34-35)
- When He returns He will wear red. (Revelations 19:13, Isaiah 63:2, Doctrine and Covenants of the Church of Jesus Christ of Latter-Day Saints section 133 verse 48)
- His hair and beard are white as snow. (Revelations 1:14)

It appears that Santa Claus is not only symbolic of Christmas, he is a similitude of the Son of God Himself.

As our children try to live the best they can all through the year in anticipation of Santa's coming, it prepares them to live worthily all their lives in anticipation of the Second Coming of the Lord Jesus Christ.

The spirit of Christmas is charity, which is the pure love of Christ. Let us have this in our hearts all the year.

When we see the loving figure dressed in red, let us see also our Lord and Saviour and remember both His birth and His imminent return.

My father's philosophy was good as far as it goes, but this is why I believe in Santa Claus.

I know who He is.

6 My Children and Santa

Remembering the feeling of betrayal when my mother lowered the boom about both the Easter Bunny and Santa Claus I vowed to always be truthful with my own children.

Our two girls grew up believing in Santa and knowing that I did also. When the time came to learn where the presents came from they also learned who I believe Santa to really be.

We learned early on that our girls were not going to go to sleep easily on Christmas Eve, and than sneaking the presents under the trce was like a special ops mission to the heart of the Kremlin. Discovery lurked at every turn and the risk of their sudden appearance in the hallway, needing a drink or a potty run, was insanely high.

I devised a fiendishly clever plan.

"I have an idea," I said to them one Christmas Eve. We had put out the cookies and milk, hung our stockings, sung carols around the tree, read the scriptural accounts of Christ's birth and written letters to Santa. We also put out our special key. This was a key with the image of Santa on it that the special visitor could use to unlock our front door (we didn't have a chimney and he had to get in **somehow**).

We would hang this key on our porch railing so it could be easily found.

In the morning the key would be resting on the empty plate where the cookies had been. Next to the plate would be answers to the letters written the night before.

As I said, on this Christmas Eve I had a brilliant idea.

"Let's go into Crystal's room (our oldest) and turn on some Christmas music, close the door and open the blinds and watch for Santa Claus."

We did. The four of us snuggled together on

Crystal's bed and watched the winter night through her window. After a few minutes I excused myself with the pretense of heading to the bathroom. I closed the door and went to my Christmas stash. I quickly put everything that I had picked up during the year under the tree and in the stockings. I then went into the bathroom and flushed the toilet.

I went back into Crystal's room. After a few minutes my wife excused herself saying she needed to get ready for bed. She put out everything she had to put out and then rejoined us.

No sneaking! No stress! No fear of discovery! It was wonderful.

Soon we sent Kelly, our youngest by three years, off to bed and my wife and I also retired.

This became a family tradition. Every year we watch for Santa out of Crystal's window.

She's married now to a wonderful husband who has wholeheartedly joined in our traditions and all five of us climb onto Crystal's bed and watch out the window.

Christ's birth was heralded by angels. Maybe our celebration of Him is also accompanied by Heavenly Messengers from time to time. This Christmas Eve, take the time to look out the window.

Who knows what you might see.

Merry Christmas and Peace on Earth, good will to all men.

About The Author

Darren Griffin is an internationally known author, key note speaker and composer, and is hard at work preparing his second music album for release.

He is a Consulting Hypnotist and teaches a variety of self help seminars and workshops. His specialties include Stress Management, Self Esteem and Eliminating the Fear of Success, Reiki, Smoking Cessation, Regression, Imprint Removal, Emergency Hypnosis, Pain Management and Forensic Hypnosis.

Darren has also been a ventriloquist since the age of eight. He now has fourteen characters and does shows all over the western United States.

He spent twenty two years in broadcasting and won six EMMYs, seven TELLYs and over twenty awards from the Utah Broadcaster's Association.

He lives in the Western United States with his wife, two daughters, one son-in-law and two ferrets.

Feel free to contact him at www.griffintalent.com.

Made in United States
North Haven, CT
27 September 2024

57698446R00026